What's in the SOUTHEAST?

By Natalie Hyde

Crabtree Publishing Company
www.crabtreebooks.com

Crabtree Publishing Company
www.crabtreebooks.com

Author: Natalie Hyde
Publishing plan research and development:
Sean Charlebois, Reagan Miller
Crabtree Publishing Company
Editor: Lynn Peppas
Proofreader: Crystal Sikkens
Editorial director: Kathy Middleton
Photo research: Crystal Sikkens
Designer: Ken Wright
Production coordinator: Ken Wright
Prepress technician: Ken Wright
Print coordinator: Katherine Berti

Cover description: A statue of Spanish explorer Ponce de León recognizes the first European expedition to Florida. The Great Smokey Mountains form the Tennessee and North Carolina border. Coal has been an economic staple of the state of Kentucky ever since the first mine was opened in 1820. The city of Nashville is the capital of the state of Tennessee and is sometimes called the "Music City" for its thriving music industry.

Title page description: A steamboat cruises down the Mississippi River.

Photographs:
The Bridgeman Art Library International: Peter Newark Western Americana: page 14 (bottom); Davies, Arthur Bowen/Private Collection: page 19 (bottom)
Dreamstime: pages 26, 27 (top), 28,
iStockphoto.com: pages 13 (top), 29 (bottom)
Photos.com: pages 22, 23 (top)
Wikimedia Commons: Jonathan Zander: page 7; Gsmith: page 15, Henry Brueckner: page 17 (left); Library of Congress: pages 20 (bottom), 21 (bottom); Doug Coldwell: page 21 (top); Sgt. Cherie A. Thurlby, USAF: page 23 (bottom); International Bird Rescue Research Center: page 25 (top); Patrick Kelley: page 25 (bottom); Jeff Kubina: page 27 (bottom)
All other images by Shutterstock.com

Illustrations:
Barbara Bedell: pages 18, 19 (top)
Samara Parent: pages 4–5, 6, 8, 24
Margaret Salter: pages 14 (top), 15 (top)
Ken Wright: pages 4–5, 6, 8, 24

Library and Archives Canada Cataloguing in Publication

Hyde, Natalie, 1963-
    What's in the Southeast? / Natalie Hyde.

(All around the U.S.)
Includes index.
Issued also in electronic formats.
ISBN 978-0-7787-1825-3 (bound).--ISBN 978-0-7787-1831-4 (pbk.)

    1. Southern States--Juvenile literature. I. Title. II. Series: All around the U.S.

F209.3.H93 2012   j975   C2011-904846-9

Library of Congress Cataloging-in-Publication Data

Hyde, Natalie, 1963-
  What's in the Southeast? / Natalie Hyde.
    p. cm. -- (All around the u.s.)
Includes index.
  ISBN 978-0-7787-1825-3 (reinforced library binding : alk. paper) -- ISBN 978-0-7787-1831-4 (pbk. : alk. paper) -- ISBN 978-1-4271-8779-6 (electronic pdf) -- ISBN 978-1-4271-9597-5 (electronic html)
  1. Southern States--Juvenile literature. I. Title. II. Series.

F209.3.H93 2012
975--dc23
                                          2011026692

Crabtree Publishing Company

Printed in Canada/082011/MA20110714

www.crabtreebooks.com   1-800-387-7650

Published in Canada
Crabtree Publishing
616 Welland Ave.
St. Catharines, ON
L2M 5V6

Published in the United States
Crabtree Publishing
PMB 59051
350 Fifth Avenue, 59th Floor
New York, New York 10118

Published in the United Kingdom
Crabtree Publishing
Maritime House
Basin Road North, Hove
BN41 1WR

Published in Australia
Crabtree Publishing
3 Charles Street
Coburg North
VIC 3058

CONTENTS

The United States of America 4

The Southeast Region 6

The Highs and Lows of the Southeast 8

Water World 10

Hot and Sunny, with a Chance of Snow? 12

Who Came First? 14

European Invasion 16

A Life of Labor 18

A Country Divided 20

City Centers 22

In the Ground 24

Come Again! 26

Song and Dance 28

Timeline 30

Find Out More 31

Glossary and Index 32

Words that are defined in the glossary are in **bold** type
the first time they appear in the text.

The United States of America

The United States is located on the **continent** of North America. It is divided into 50 states and the District of Columbia. To the north it borders Canada, and Mexico is on the southern border. To the west is the Pacific Ocean and to the east, the Atlantic Ocean. It is the third largest country by size in the world. The landscape ranges from mountains and forests, to plains, deserts, and tropical beaches.

Over and Above

The only two states not connected to the mainland are Alaska, north of Canada, and Hawaii, which is in the Pacific Ocean.

REGIONS

The United States is divided into regions. A region is an area that shares the same features. Regions can be based on landforms, cultures, languages, and habitats. Regions can be as big as a group of states or as small as a city. Regions are a way for people to describe a place that has common features. In this series, the United States is divided into five major regions: the Northeast, the Southeast, the Midwest, the Southwest, and the West. Each region is named for its geographic location. Each region is made up of states that are close together.

The Southeast Region

The Southeast Region of the United States is rich in culture and history. It is home to **endangered** animals, the world's largest cave system, and the oldest continuously occupied settlement in the country. The land sweeps up into mountain ranges from coastal plains and wetlands. The Mississippi River, which flows through the Southeast, is the largest river in the country. This area has always been densely populated because of the mild climate and abundance of farmland. Native Americans lived inland where there was good hunting and farming. Later, Europeans from France, Germany and Spain settled in the area.

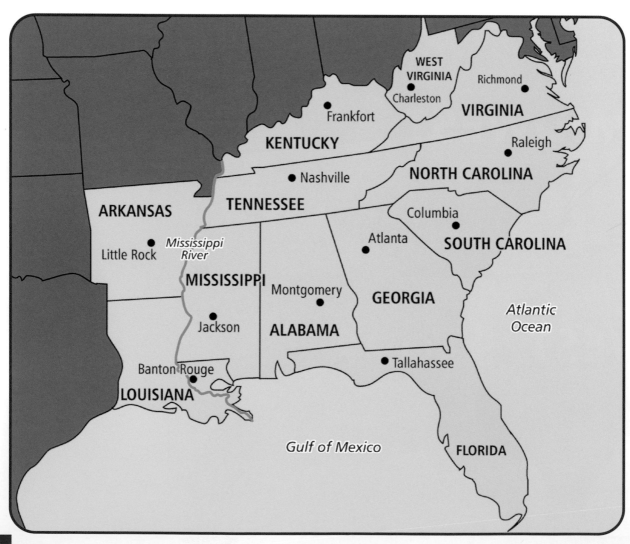

HISTORY OF THE REGION

There are twelve states in the Southeast Region. Virginia, North Carolina, South Carolina, and Georgia are four of the original thirteen colonies. Florida has the most people of any state in the Southeast. Kentucky is one of only four states known as a "Commonwealth." They use the term Commonwealth of Kentucky to stress that their government was formed by the will of the people living there. Louisiana is the only state to be divided into "parishes" instead of counties. The French and Spanish Roman Catholics who settled there referred to different sections by the name of the church or parish that served the area. When Louisiana entered the Union, they kept this system. The remaining states in the Southeast are Alabama, Arkansas, Mississippi, Tennessee, and West Virginia.

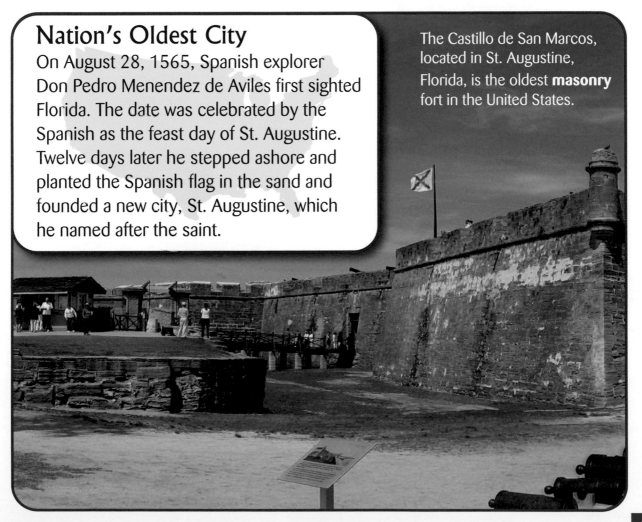

Nation's Oldest City

On August 28, 1565, Spanish explorer Don Pedro Menendez de Aviles first sighted Florida. The date was celebrated by the Spanish as the feast day of St. Augustine. Twelve days later he stepped ashore and planted the Spanish flag in the sand and founded a new city, St. Augustine, which he named after the saint.

The Castillo de San Marcos, located in St. Augustine, Florida, is the oldest **masonry** fort in the United States.

The Highs and Lows of the Southeast

The Southeast has a variety of landforms. A landform is any natural formation on Earth's surface. Hills, valleys, plateaus, plains, and mountains are all types of landforms that can be found in the Southeast.

SUB-REGIONS

The Appalachian Mountain Range is one of the oldest mountain ranges in the world. It runs through eight states in the Southeast Region. Sections of the mountain range are known as the Great Smoky Mountains, or "Smokies," and the Blue Ridge Mountains. The highest peak is Mount Mitchell in North Carolina.

Blue and Smoky

Both the Great Smoky Mountains and Blue Ridge Mountains are covered with hardwood trees. In hot weather these trees release a chemical into the air called isoprene, which creates a blue or smoky haze.

(below) The Smokies are part of the Blue Ridge Mountains, so they sometimes look both blue and smoky.

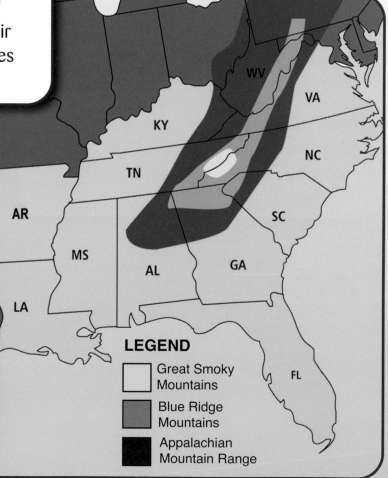

LEGEND

- Great Smoky Mountains
- Blue Ridge Mountains
- Appalachian Mountain Range

THE GREAT VALLEY

In the center of the Appalachian mountain system is a series of valleys making a long **trough** from Quebec, Canada to Alabama. The Great Valley has been a north-south route for thousands of years. These valley lowlands also have fertile land for growing crops and raising livestock.

PIEDMONT

Between the Appalachian Mountains and the sea is the Piedmont. In French, piedmont roughly translates into (pied) foot (mont) hill. These foothills were once a large mountain range that have eroded over millions of years creating rolling hills.

UNDERGROUND

Below the ground in south central Kentucky lies a vast cave system. The Mammoth Caves are the longest cave system in the world, over 390 miles (628 km)! Native Americans gathered minerals from the caves thousands of years ago and left behind mussel shells, gourds, and cane torches.

Since 1816, visitors have been able to tour the spectacular Mammoth Caves.

Water World

The Southeast has many wetlands that are an important part of the **ecosystem**. Not only are wetlands home to many types of birds and animals, but they also act as a filter to remove pollutants from the water.

BAYOUS AND EVERGLADES

The coastal plains of the Southeast Region often contain swamps and marshes known as bayous and the everglades. These areas have slow moving, or **stagnant** water and the trees, shrubs, and grasses have adapted to living in a wet environment.

MANGROVES

The Florida mangroves off the south coast are an ecosystem of trees that live in salt water. These mangrove trees provide a nursery for young fish like

snappers, angelfish, and barracuda. The branches of mangroves are roosts and nests for birds such as cormorants and herons.

Animals such as these eagle rays and heron use the mangroves to find homes, shelter, and to raise their young.

SALT MARSHES

Salt marshes are formed in coastal plains next to salt water. The Mississippi Delta marshes are teeming with life. It supplies important nesting and brooding habitat for shorebirds, wading birds, and marsh birds. **Migratory** birds use the delta as a stopover on the way south in fall or north in spring. Here they can rest and eat plenty of fish, frogs, and crayfish to gain strength for the rest of their journey.

BARRIER ISLANDS

Barrier islands are narrow strips of sand parallel to the coast. They are found where there are low tides and a gently sloping underwater shelf. The barrier islands provide most of the nesting grounds for birds such as pelicans, herons, terns, and gulls.

The Great River Road
The Mississippi River was formed after the last ice age, when massive glaciers that had carved out the river basin began to melt and the water drained to the sea. At 2,350 miles (3,782 km) long, it is the fourth longest river in the world!

Hot and Sunny, with a Chance of Snow?

The Southeast is known for its mild winters and warm summers. The climate for the region is very different on the coastal plains than it is in the Appalachian Mountains. Climate is the average weather for an area over a long period of time.

COASTAL PLAINS

The warm ocean currents keep the climate on the coastal plains mild and warm. Here the temperature rarely goes below freezing, even in winter. The long growing season is perfect for crops such as peanuts and **citrus fruits**.

PIEDMONT PLATEAU

The piedmont plateau has milder weather than the mountains, but it still gets about ten inches of snow in winter. The growing season is shorter than on the coastal plains because it is closer to the mountains and farther from the warming effect of the ocean.

Florida has one of the best climates for growing citrus fruits, such as oranges. Ninety percent of all the orange juice consumed in the U.S. comes from Florida oranges.

MOUNTAINS

In the mountains the weather can change quickly from sun to snow in a few hours. Depending on the height of a mountain, the temperature can be 20 degrees different from the base to the top of a mountain. In the winter it is very cold and there is heavy snow.

The Blue Ridge Mountains and Lake Burnett in North Carolina

HURRICANE ALERT!

The same warm water that keeps the winters mild in the Southeast are also responsible for some extreme weather. Hurricanes develop over water and have strong winds and heavy rains.

Naming a hurricane

Each year hurricanes are named with a different letter of the alphabet starting with A. (Q, U, X, Y, and Z are never used.) There are six rotating lists of names. After six years, the first list is used again. After a particularly severe or damaging hurricane, the name is retired.

After the devastating Hurricane Katrina in 2005, the name "Katrina" was retired and replaced with "Katia."

Who Came First?

Thousands of years ago the Southeast Region was home to many different Native Americans. Some of these tribes were the most advanced civilizations in the Americas. They built villages, were skillful farmers, and sculpted huge mounds as temples.

CHEROKEE

According to Cherokee legends, early Cherokee people left the Great Lakes Region and traveled south. They settled in North Carolina where there were a lot of animals to hunt and fertile valleys to plant **maize**, beans, and squash. They did well and the Cherokee Nation grew. At one time it covered all or parts of Georgia, North Carolina, South Carolina, Kentucky, Alabama, Tennessee, Virginia, and West Virginia.

The Trail of Tears

In 1830 the government moved many Native nations, including the Cherokee and the Choctaw, to new **reservations** in the west. The walk there was long and difficult. Many Native Americans died along the way. The route was given the name "Trail of Tears."

SEMINOLE

The Seminole made their home in the Florida everglades. They built small villages with a central eating house where everyone ate together. Although they planted some crops such as pumpkins, paw paws, and corn, they were not farmers. They moved often following the fish, alligators, turtles, and wild fruit and vegetables such as mangos, guava, and oranges that made up their diet.

The Seminole often built homes called chickees. Chickees had thatched roofs made from leaves or plants. The sides were left open to allow breezes to easily flow through.

NATCHEZ

The Natchez who lived along the Mississippi River were a bit of a mystery. They spent years building steep, dirt packed platforms to communicate with the Great Spirit. The mounds could be as large as three football fields. Some were only a few feet high, but others soared to 70 feet (21 m) tall!

Ancestors of the Natchez constructed the Emerald mound for ceremonial rituals as well. It is now a National Historic site. The mound stands 35 feet (11 m) high and spreads across eight acres (3.2 hectares).

European Invasion

When Ponce de Leon sighted a new coastline in 1513, it was the Easter season, which in Spain is called Pascua Florida (the Festival of Flowers). He named this new land, La Florida. Forty years later, French and Spanish colonists arrived and small settlements were built. Eventually, the Spanish took control of the area and began expanding northward. Their influence can still be seen in building styles and town names such as Boca Raton (Mouse Mouth) and Del Rio (From the River).

FRENCH SETTLERS

The French arrived in the Southeast Region from the north where they had established a large fur-trading network in the Great Lakes area. They began traveling down the Mississippi River, and eventually settled in the lower Mississippi River valley. More French settlers came when the Acadians were driven out of the Maritime provinces in Canada. They put down roots in Louisiana where the name "Acadian" became "Cajun."

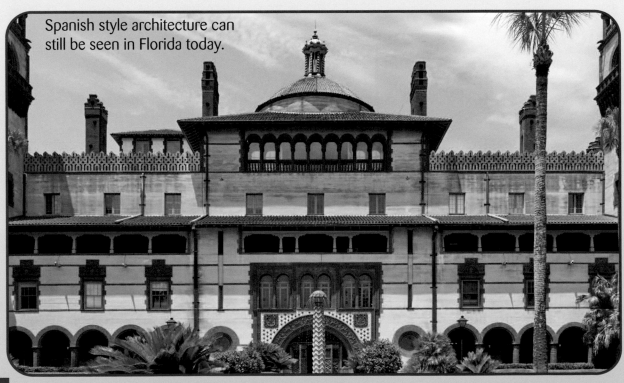
Spanish style architecture can still be seen in Florida today.

THE BRITISH

The British also wanted a share of the riches of the Southeast. They sent ships with 104 settlers to establish the "Virginia English **Colony**" on the banks of the James River. Between the hostile Algonquian Native Americans, starvation, and disease they had a difficult time and many settlers died. The colony managed to survive with new supplies from England, and John Rolfe's marriage to Pocahontas, the daughter of an Algonquian chief.

FIRST INDEPENDENCE

Virginia, along with three Southeastern neighbors of Georgia and North and South Carolina, became four of the original 13 states to declare independence from England and form the United States.

(left) Pocahontas married John Rolfe in 1614.

The Fountain of Youth

Legend says that when Ponce de Leon (right) discovered Florida, he was actually looking for the fabled "Fountain of Youth." The water from this spring was supposed to restore youth and health to anyone who drank it. Too bad Ponce de Leon did not find it. On his second visit to Florida he was shot with a poisoned arrow and died from his wound.

A Life of Labor

Another large ethnic group arrived in the Southeast Region, but not by choice. From the 1600s to the 1800s, hundreds of thousands of people were captured from the west coast of Africa and brought to the Americas as slaves.

Slaves spent long hours in the hot sun working on plantations, like this cotton field.

SLAVE LABOR

Slaves were brought to the Southeast Region to work on large cotton and tobacco **plantations**. Harvesting these crops required a lot of labor and landowners used slaves to work the fields rather than paying to hire workers. Slaves were bought and sold and considered to be property. They were often treated cruelly.

cotton plant

tobacco plant

AFRICAN AMERICANS

Over the years, many generations of Africans were born and raised in the Southeast. After slavery was **abolished** at the end of the Civil War, most African Americans settled in the areas where they had worked and lived. Even though their freedom was granted in 1865, their struggle for equality continues.

The Underground Railroad

Before slavery was abolished, many slaves fled from the plantations and tried to head north to freedom. They traveled at night, looking for houses, called stations, with a lit lantern hanging outside on a pole. This was a sign that it was safe for them to stay. People who were against slavery helped runaway slaves by providing food, clothing, and safe places to hide along the way.

Harriet Tubman was a slave who escaped and then made 19 trips back to the Southeast to escort more slaves to freedom.

People against slavery helped runaway slaves hide from slave owners.

A Country Divided

The American Civil War that split the country in two and cost thousands of lives took place mostly in the Southeast. Major battles were fought in every state in the Southeast.

CAUSE OF WAR

The Southeast states were part of the **Confederacy** that wanted to separate from the rest of the country. The Union Army of the North fought to keep the country united. One major dividing point was the issue of slavery. Slavery was illegal in the northern states, but landowners in the south wanted to continue with the practice.

Union flag   Confederate flag

The Battle of Stones River, also known as the Battle of Murfreesboro, was fought in Tennessee. It was one of the bloodiest battles of the Civil War.

ADVANTAGES

The Confederate Army had a huge advantage with most of the battles taking place in the Southeast. They knew the land well and this helped them in planning attacks. The Union Army, however, had more men and better supplies. Over 600,000 men lost their lives in the fighting and many are buried in the Southeast.

END OF CIVIL WAR

In April 1865, after four years of fierce battles, General Robert E. Lee of the Confederate Army surrendered at Appomattox Court House, Virginia. This site is now a National Historic Site, along with many other Civil War sites.

(below) Peace terms are copied after General Robert E. Lee surrenders to Union army leader General Ulysses S. Grant at the Appomattox Court House (right).

The Mason Dixon Line

This famous line is remembered as the divider between the north and the south, slavery and freedom. Charles Mason and Jeremiah Dixon actually surveyed the line to settle a land dispute between two families. Mason and Dixon used stars to calculate the boundary line and placed huge blocks of limestone brought over from England at one-mile intervals.

Robert E. Lee

Ulysses S. Grant

City Centers

The mild climate and new job opportunities in the Southeast are just some of the reasons that the population is growing in this region.

RETIREES

Many retirees are moving to southern states such as Florida, Georgia, and North and South Carolina, especially in counties along the coast. New communities are being built so people can take advantage of the warm winters and recreation in the area.

JACKSONVILLE

Jacksonville, Florida is the largest city in the Southeast Region. It was originally called Fort Caroline by the French. It was later conquered by the Spanish and then handed over to the British. It is an important settlement because it has a deep, protected port and it is located at a key crossing of the St. John River. In the 1940s, three naval bases were built there.

Over 800,000 people live in the city of Jacksonville, Florida.

CHARLOTTE

Charlotte, North Carolina, had its first growth spurt in 1799 when a large chunk of gold was found. This set off a gold rush in the area and the town grew to supply **prospectors**. Today, job seekers come to work in finance because Charlotte has become the second largest banking center in the United States.

TENNESSEE

Both Tennessee cities of Memphis and Nashville are known for music. Blues and Rock and Roll got their start in Memphis with stars such as Elvis Presley and B. B. King. Nashville attracts country music stars to its many clubs and bars and is home to the Grand Ole Opry.

(left) Shown here is the financial district in Charlotte, North Carolina.

(bottom) By way of a live video feed, U.S. soldiers in Iraq get to watch famous country singer, Dolly Parton, sing at the Grand Ole Opry.

In the Ground

The Southeast is an area rich in **natural resources**. Mining, oil production, timber, and agriculture have all helped shape the region.

COAL

The Appalachian Mountains have large coal deposits and the mines once produced two-thirds of the country's coal. Today, underground mines have largely been replaced with surface mining. Many groups are protesting the destruction of the Appalachian Mountains in search of coal.

Workers move coal at a processing facility in Kentucky.

AGRICULTURE

Agriculture has always been a major source of income in the southeast. The warm climate and long growing season make it the perfect spot for citrus fruits, such as oranges and grapefruit, and legumes, such as peanuts.

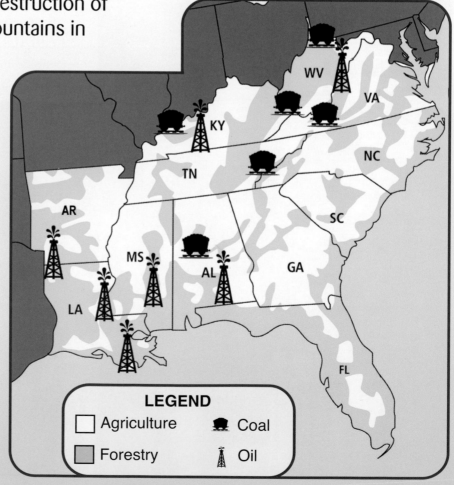

LEGEND

Agriculture   Coal

Forestry   Oil

OIL

Oil is a non-renewable resource found in the Southeast Region. Non-renewable resources are materials that cannot be re-grown or replaced in nature. Kentucky and West Virginia are big producers of oil, but offshore in the Gulf of Mexico, new oil **reservoirs** are being discovered.

INDUSTRY

Industry in the Southeast has been changing. There is a boom in technology with research parks and communications. Major networks such as CNN and the Cartoon Network are located in the Southeast. Other industries are growing as well, such as automobile manufacturing with BMW and Mercedes-Benz.

Crisis!

The Gulf Oil Spill was a disaster that affected the economy and the environment in the Southeast. Hundreds of birds and animals died in the sticky mess. Under the water, the lack of sunlight and chemicals in the water affected all parts of the food chain in the ecosystem. It may be decades before nature can recover.

Workers clean oil off a pelican (above) and a beach (below) in Louisiana after the Deepwater Horizon oil rig exploded.

Come Again!

The Southeast is a popular destination for tourists. The weather, the recreation, and the attractions draw millions of people each year.

WALT DISNEY WORLD

Tourism is Florida's main industry. Students flock to the beaches of the **Florida panhandle** to enjoy spring break. There are many theme parks such as Walt Disney World, which is a favorite vacation for families.

MAMMOTH CAVES

Before the Mammoth Caves became a National Park in 1941, several families joined in the "Kentucky Cave Wars." They tried to lure tourists to privately owned caves or entrances to the Mammoth Caves on their land. Now, the cave system and the area surrounding it is protected. In 1981 it became a World Heritage Site.

A Cast of Thousands

It takes around 62,000 people working at Walt Disney World to create the magic for visitors. It employs more people than any other site in the United States.

APPALACHIAN TRAIL

The Appalachian National Scenic Trail is a 2,175-mile (3,500 km) long public hiking trail. It crosses five states in the Southeast: West Virginia, Virginia, North Carolina, Tennessee, and Georgia. Over four million people enjoy the trail each year.

(above) The Appalachian Trail runs from Maine to Georgia.

(below) The Kentucky Derby is always on the first Saturday in May.

KENTUCKY DERBY

The Kentucky Derby opened in 1875 and is known as "The Greatest Two Minutes in Sport." It is the longest running annual sporting event in America. More than 150,000 people watch the spectacular horse race at Churchill Downs racetrack.

CIVIL WAR RE-ENACTMENTS

Thousands of people enjoy watching or participating in Civil War Re-enactments. These events are held at many different battle sites in the Southeast and usually take place over a weekend. The re-enactors spend a lot of time and money recreating the actual battles in **authentic** costumes.

Song and Dance

The Southeast Region has a **diverse** culture. The Native Americans, early Europeans, and African Americans have all played a part in influencing art, literature, customs, and music in the area.

POWWOW

The Powwow is a Native American celebration. Drummers provide the music for dancers dressed in colorful costumes. Welcome songs, grass-dances, crow-hops, and sneak-up songs are some of the performances put on for spectators. Native artwork on jewelry, baskets, pottery, and paintings are prized by collectors.

CAJUN CULTURE

Cajun culture is unique in the world. The French Acadians from the Canadian provinces of Nova Scotia, New Brunswick, and Prince Edward Island settled in Louisiana after being forced out from their homes. Today, Cajuns are well known for their food, music, and festivals. Musicians typically use the accordion, fiddle, and triangle to play Cajun music.

Native Americans at the Trail of Tears Powwow in Hopkinsville, KY, perform traditional dances for the audience.

AFRICAN CULTURE

Many parts of African culture were passed down by slaves through storytelling, song, and dance. Blues, jazz, and hip hop are only some of the musical styles influenced by African American culture. Soul food is a style of cooking mainly in the Southeast that uses local foods to make hearty, filling dishes such as cornbread, ham hocks, and fried greens.

(above) Hoppin' John is a southern dish made from black-eyed peas and rice.

(below) In a New Orleans Mardi Gras parade, people on the floats throw colored beads to the spectators.

Fat Tuesday

Mardi Gras (Fat Tuesday in French) is a Roman Catholic celebration in many southern cities that includes parties and parades. In New Orleans, as many as a half a million people line the parade route.

Timeline

20,000 B.C. – Native American tribes live in the Southeast

1513 – Ponce de Leon lands in Florida

1562 – French settle Fort Carolina, Florida

1565 – St. Augustine, Florida is founded

1607 – First settlers arrive in Jamestown, Virginia

1619 – First African slaves arrive on a Dutch slave ship

1781 – American Revolution ends, United States declares Independence

1799 – First piece of gold found in North Carolina, starting a gold rush

1831 – Relocation of Native Americans and Trail of Tears begins

1837 – The first Mardi Gras parade in New Orleans

1861 – The Civil War begins

1863 – The Emancipation Proclamation is passed, freeing slaves

1875 – First Kentucky Derby

1865 – The Civil War ends

1923 – The first section of the Appalachian Trail opens

1964 – Civil Rights laws end separation for African Americans

1971 – Walt Disney World opens in Florida

1981 – Mammoth Caves becomes a World Heritage Site

2005 – Hurricane Katrina hits the Gulf coast, causing damage from Florida to Texas

2010 – Deepwater Horizon oil spill damages coastlines and marine life in the Gulf of Mexico

Find Out More

BOOKS

The Unofficial Guide to the Southeast with Kids. King, Sehlinger, Mize and Worrel, John Wiley & Sons, 2000.

Frederick Douglass: *From Slavery to Statesman*. Henry Elliot, Crabtree, 2009

Soft Rain: *A Story of the Cherokee Trail of Tears*. Cornelia Cornelissen, Yearling, 1999

Minn of the Mississippi. Holling C. Holling, Sandpiper, 1978.

The Rag Coat. Lauren A. Mills, Little, Brown Books for Young Readers, 1991.

WEBSITES

Learn about the different Southeast Woodland tribes:
http://nativeamericans.mrdonn.org/southeast.html

Flat Stanley travels on the Appalachian Trail:
http://rohland.homedns.org/at/flatstanley/menuflatstanley.asp

History for Kids explores the American Civil War:
www.historyforkids.org/learn/northamerica/after1500/history/civilwar.htm

Learn about mangroves:
www.globio.org/glossopedia/article.aspx?art_id=39

Glossary

abolished To do away with completely

authentic Made or done in the traditional or original way

citrus fruit Fruit such as oranges and lemons that have a thick rind and juicy pulp

colony An area under control of another country and occupied by settlers from that country

confederacy A league of states joined together by agreement

continent A large landmass on Earth

diverse Different from one another

ecosystem A community of living things and their environment

endangered At risk of disappearing from the face of Earth

Florida Panhandle The narrow strip of land in Florida between Alabama and the Gulf of Mexico

maize Indian corn

migratory Animals that move with the seasons

natural resources Materials such as minerals, forests, and water that occur in nature and can be used to make money

plantation An estate where crops such as coffee, tobacco, or cotton are grown and harvested

prospector Someone who explores an area for minerals

reservation An area of land set aside for the use of Native Americans

reservoir A large lake used as a source of water supply

stagnant Having no current or flow, often having an unpleasant smell as a result

trough A long, narrow area

Index

agriculture 9, 12, 14, 15, 18, 24

Appalachian Mountains 8, 9, 12, 13, 27

cities 7, 22, 23

Civil War 19, 20, 21, 27

climate/weather 12, 13, 26

coastal plains 6, 12

culture 28, 29

food 14, 15, 29

Kentucky Derby 27

landscape 4, 5, 6, 8, 9

Mammoth Caves 6, 9, 26

Mardi Gras 29

Mason Dixon Line 21

Mississippi River 6, 11, 15, 16

music 23, 28, 29

Native Americans 6, 9, 14, 15, 17, 28

natural resources 24, 25

piedmont 9, 12

Ponce de Leon 16, 17

population 22, 23

slavery 18, 19, 20

tourism 26, 27

wetlands 6, 10, 11